Mel Bay's
Celtic Tune
ENCYCLOPEDIA

for 5-String Banjo

by Iain E. MacLachlan

MW00813286

1 2 3 4 5 6 7 8 9 0

Visit us on the Web at www.melbay.com — E-mail us at email@melbay.com

Table of Contents

Preface

The aim of this book is to bring another strand of music to the 5 string banjo. The mainstay of most banjo pickers is probably bluegrass and I am no exception. The movement out from this starting point into other styles is well documented and has pushed the boundaries of what people expect from the 5-string banjo. This book in some ways takes the music back a step from bluegrass to the music of Scotland and Ireland. Bill Monroe was proud of his Scottish roots so it is only fitting that Scottish music should return to it's place in the repertoire of banjo players.

It is already there in spirit and in some of the everyday tunes that we all like to play. The influence of Scottish settlers and the music they brought with them is undeniable. You only have to look at the number of Pipe bands all over the world to see some of the influence and this book includes a number of pipe tunes for you to try. I wonder, if we could get a hundred banjo players to march down Main Street, all playing in unison, would it be as fearsome a sound as a hundred bagpipers?

I have played Scottish tunes ever since first learning the banjo here in Edinburgh. However it wasn't until I started playing for dance classes and then with The Thunderdog Ceilidh Band that I really got to grips with the music. Because my work is for dancing the tunes are arranged in sets of a specific length. A set is a medley of tunes which are played together for the duration of the dance. Sets can of course be made up of tunes with differing rhythms and timings if they are for listening rather than dancing. It is also possible to change from reel time into jig time during a dance without interfering with the timing, thus giving a different feel to the dancers. If the dancers stop and stare it's not because they are amazed at your playing!

Because of the change of keys associated with a lot of the sets and even within some of the individual tunes, there is no place for the capo or retuning the banjo. This will hopefully expand your knowledge of the fingerboard and give you new insights into other ways of playing the music you already know. A lot of the tunes are in the keys of A and D which are the fiddler's favourite keys it seems. Bagpipes play in Bb (when they are tuned to concert pitch!) but fortunately for the rest of us few of their tunes are written in that key! I have played with bagpipers but it isn't easy! Usually I stand well back and admire them from a safe distance.

This book contains reels, jigs, polkas, strathspeys, marches, schottisches, hornpipes and waltzes. During a typical Ceilidh you can expect to play most, if not all, of these different styles. The tempos depend on the dance in progress and the age and ability of the dancers. The Royal Scottish Country Dance Society have strict rules on tempos for dancing but the Ceilidh dance is much more informal. If the dancers look like they are in a hurry, you are playing too fast! If they look bored, you are probably too slow! If you are playing for people to listen to you, then play from the heart! Most of all enjoy it. I've seen too many bands with long faces in concentration. They might be enjoying themselves but it is hard to tell!

Introduction

I use the tabs in this book when working with the Thunderdog Ceilidh Band. We principally play for dances having formed the band specifically for that reason. Because of this the sets and tunes are of a length to suit particular dances which are popular at the ceilidhs we play for. The word "ceilidh" means a gathering of people. It can be in someone's home or it can be in a hall or pub or even outdoors. Basically it is an interaction between people. Inviting a few friends round for a meal and conversation is a ceilidh. Traditional Ceilidhs will include music, dance, singing and storytelling. However, when I talk about a ceilidh in this book I am referring to a dance.

The fingering for each tab is put there as a guide only. This is the way that I play the tune but you may find another way which suits you better. I do change my mind from time to time anyway, so feel free to experiment. I always considered myself to be a Scruggs style player, having taught myself from the Earl Scruggs book. Because of this I try to get as many rolls in to the tune rather than play a single string style. There are times when the single string approach is the only option or the best way to get a certain phrase. I still find that the use of alternating strings gives a much better tone and gives the music more freedom to flow. The tunes probably can be played in a completely single string style which will make it sound more like the tenor banjo.

When I first started playing for dance classes I didn't know many Scottish tunes and used the bluegrass tunes I did know. Tunes like Blackberry Blossom, Bill Cheatham and Cripple Creek fit in with the rhythm of Scottish music. My biggest problems as I progressed on to more and more tunes were twofold. Playing the tune exactly the same way every time was something I had spent years trying to avoid! Now I had to concentrate on playing the same notes at the same time as the fiddle. The other obstacle I found was changing from one tune to the next. I have played medleys before but this was different. Usually as the tune changes so does the key. There are also times where the timing changes too. There are dances which start as Strathspeys and end as Reels. This still takes a lot of concentration on my part. There is also the problem of lead in notes. In some sets you have to miss them out because the previous tune ends on the last beat of the bar leaving no time for a lead in. However, when you play the tune for the second time you have to include the lead in.

The Sets

Reel Sets
Deveron Reel - Timour the Tartar - Dick Gossip - Aly's Soond
Mrs MacLeod - De'il Amang the Tailors - Staten Island - The Mason's Apron
The Flowers of Edinburgh - The Merry Blacksmith - Temperance Reel or The Teetotaller's Reel - Thunderdog Reel
Jack Daniel's Reel - Molly Rankine's Reel - Dinkie Dorians - The Barrowburn Reel
The Drunken Piper - Johnny Cope - My Love She's but a Lassie Yet - Lord Randolph's Bride
The Duke of Perth - Lady MacKenzie of Coull - Glengarry's March - East Neuk of Fife
Jackie Coleman's Reel - Drowsy Maggie - Willafjord - St Anne's Reel
The Sally Gardens - The Maid Behind the Bar - The New High Level - The Hamilton Rant or Dr Bob Smith
The Dashing White Sergeant - Niel Gow's Farewell to Whisky - This is no my Ain Lassie - Bonnie Prince Charlie

Jig Sets
Shandon Bells - Sweet Biddy Daly - The Tenpenny Bit - Humours of Glendart
The Jig Run Rig - Scarce o' Tatties - The Kesh Jig - The Boys of Ballymote
Swallowtail Jig - Cornerhouse Jig - The Geese in the Bog - Morrison's Jig
Jig of Slurs - The Athole Highlanders - Paddy's Leather Breeches - Lark in the Morning

Hornpipe Set
The Boys of Bluehill - The Gypsies - Chief O'Neill's Favourite - Trumpet Hornpipe

March Sets
Scotland the Brave - A Man's a Man for a' That - The Barren Rocks of Aden - The High Road to Linton
Captain Norman Orr-Ewing - Flett from Flotta - Pipe Major Donald Maclean of Lewis
Pipe Major Jim Christie of Wick - The Balkan Hills
Ballochgyle - Macleod of Mull
Glendaruel Highlanders - Murdo MacKenzie of Torridon
The Man from Skye - Crossing the Minch

Schottische
Loudon's Bonnie Woods - Kafoozalum - The Keel Row - Orange and Blue

Two Steps
Shetland Two Step - Looking for a Partner
Frank Jamieson Two Step

Polka
The Patchwork Polka

Waltz Set
The Dark Island - The House of MacDonald

Strathspey Set
Cameron's Got His Wife Again - Highland Whisky - Jessie Smith - The Piper o' Dundee

March, Strathspey and Reel
The Sprig of Ivy - J. F. MacKenzie of Garrynahine - The Apple Tree

Extra tunes
Reels
Breakdown - Circassian Circle - The Brolum - Jenny Dang the Weavers - The Shetland Fiddler - Lord MacDonald's Reel - Sleep Soond Ida Morning - The Reconciliation - Tongadale Reel - Rachel Rae - Goodnight and Joy be With You - Tarbolton Lodge

Jigs
Haste to the Wedding - Skattery Island

Marches
The Muckin' o' Geordie's Byre - Bonnie Dundee - Aros Park

Hornpipe
The Mathematician

Strathspeys
The Smith's a Gallant Fireman - The Sweetness of Mary

Song
Loch Lomond

Techniques for Playing the Tunes

Because the tunes in this book are played without a capo you will need to familiarize yourself with different positions on the neck. A lot of fiddle tunes are played in the keys of D and A so a good starting point is to become familiar with the note positions of these keys. There is only one note difference between the G and D scales - C and C♯, and one note difference between the D and A scales - G and G♯. There are different ways of playing the scales and you should spend some time finding the different ways of getting the notes. A few examples are below but are by no means the only way.

D scales

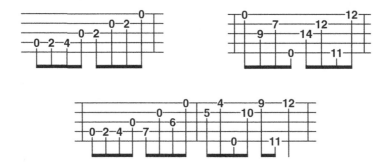

A scales

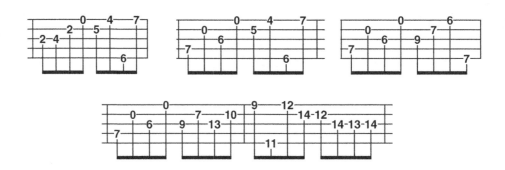

You will find many examples of single string playing in the tunes, especially on the fourth string.

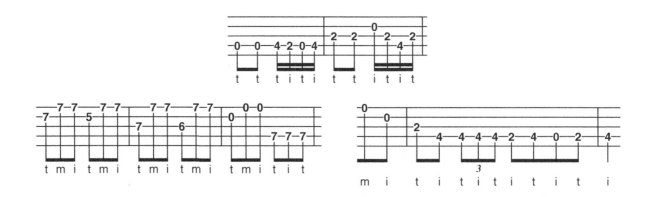

You will also find examples of what has become known as the Scottish Snap. This appears in Marches and Strathspeys where the first note of a pair is shorter than the second. For example

To play this you need to ignore the exact classical rhythm! The first note is as short as you can make it and the second note is expanded correspondingly. A friend of mine describes it as stealing from the first note and adding the time on to the following note. I can usually spot a classically trained player by this as they are playing the music exactly as written instead of getting the feel of the music.

Reels

A view from the Bridge over the Atlantic on the west coast of Scotland

Deveron Reel

Composed by Neil Grant

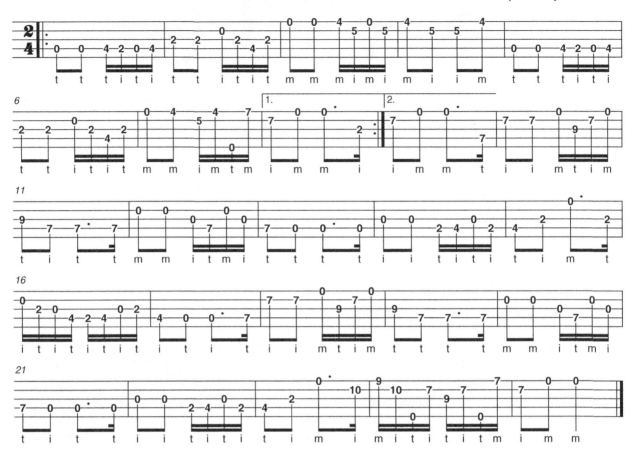

Timour the Tartar

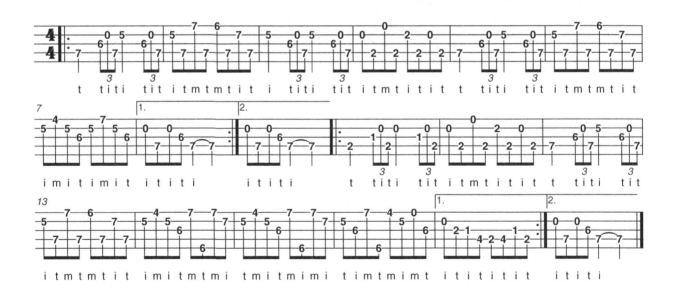

Dick Gossip

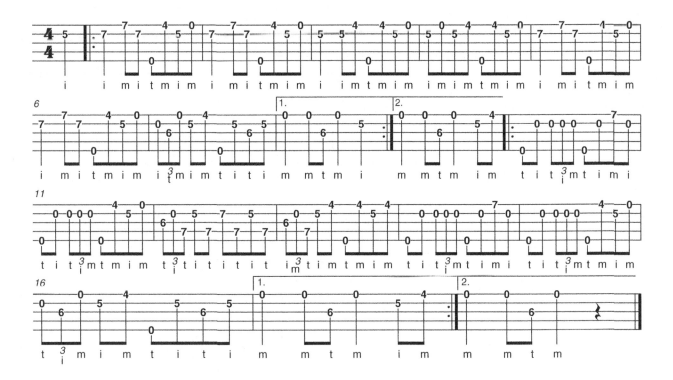

Aly's Soond

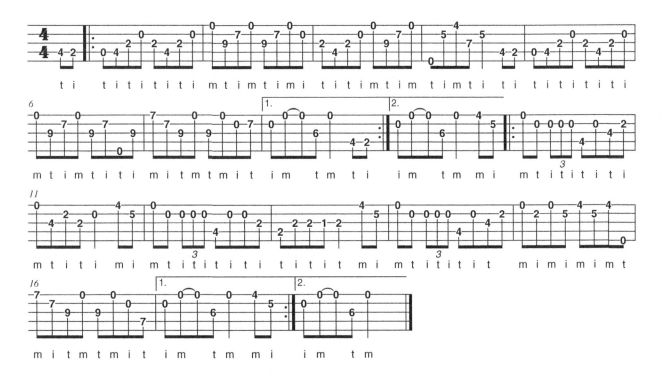

Mrs MacLeod

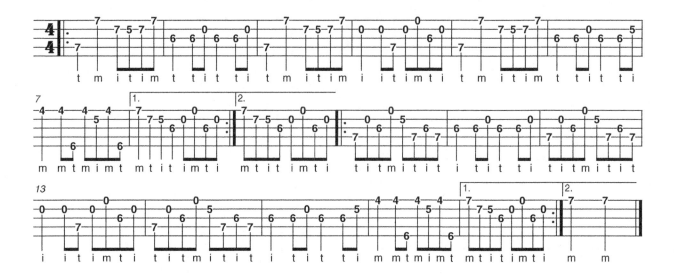

De'il Amang the Tailors

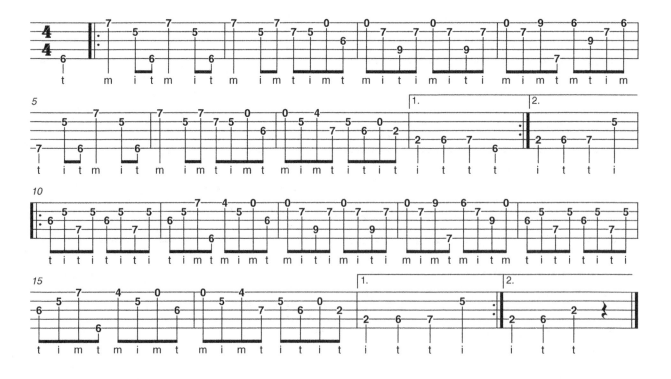

Staten Island

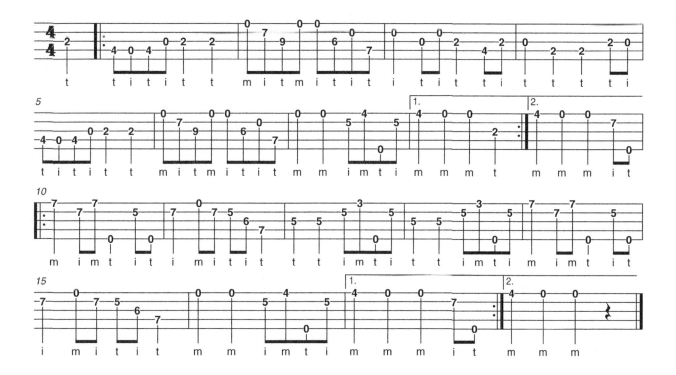

The Mason's Apron

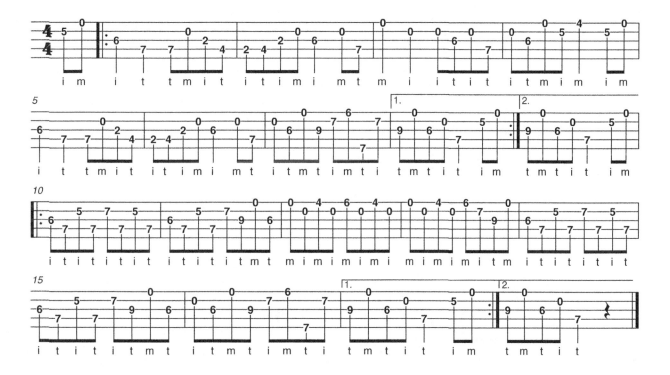

The Flowers of Edinburgh

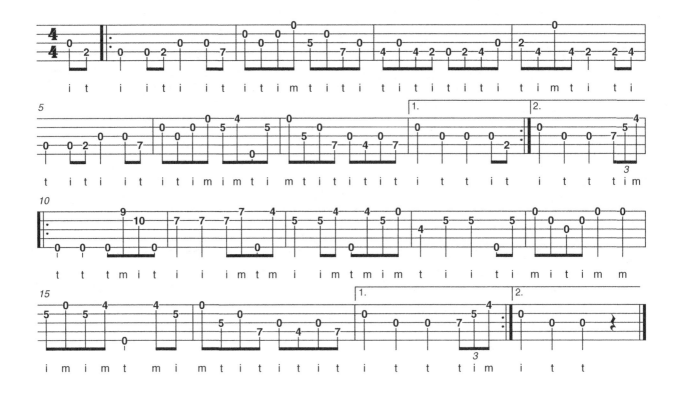

The Merry Blacksmith

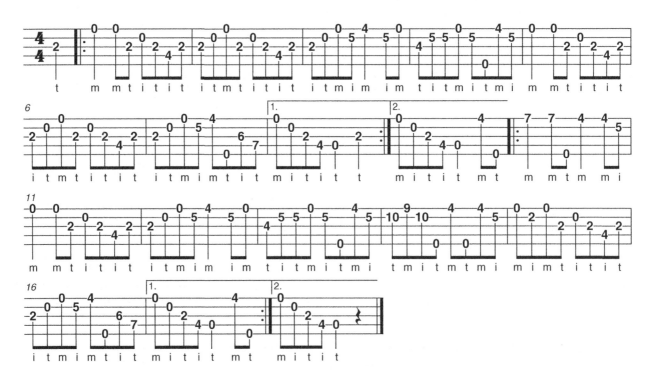

Temperence Reel or Teetotallers Reel

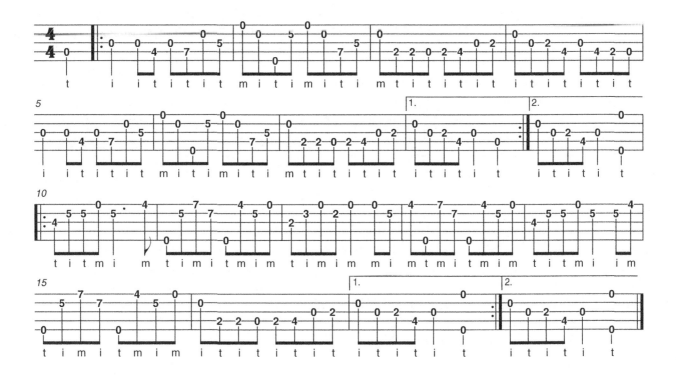

The Thunderdog Reel

Composed by Iain E. MacLachlan

Jack Daniel's Reel

John Morris Rankine

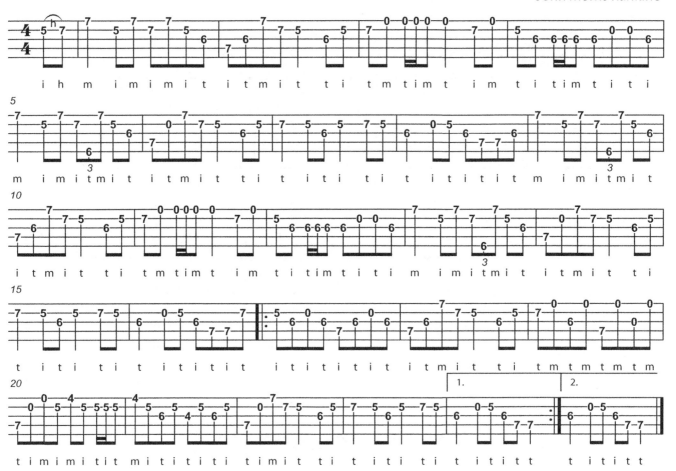

Molly Rankine

John Morris Rankine

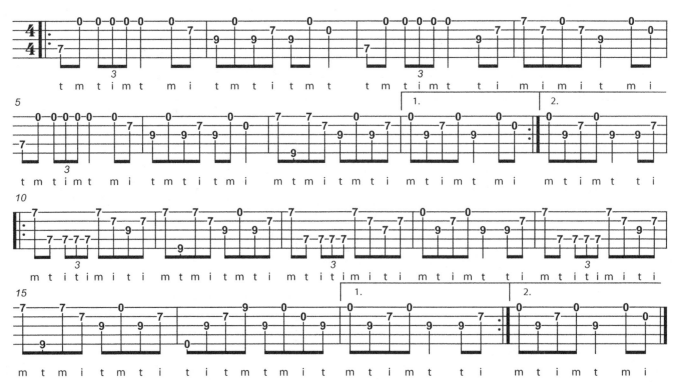

Dinkie Dorians

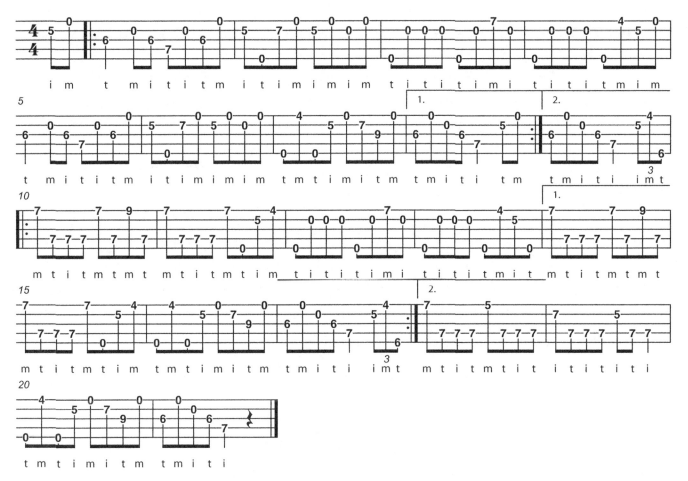

The Barrowburn Reel

Composed by Addie Harper

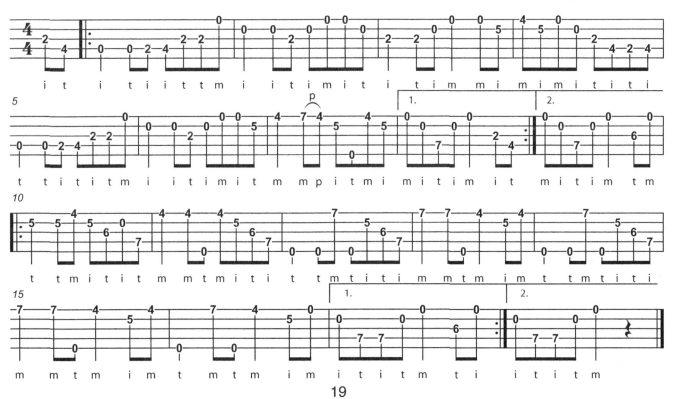

19

The Drunken Piper

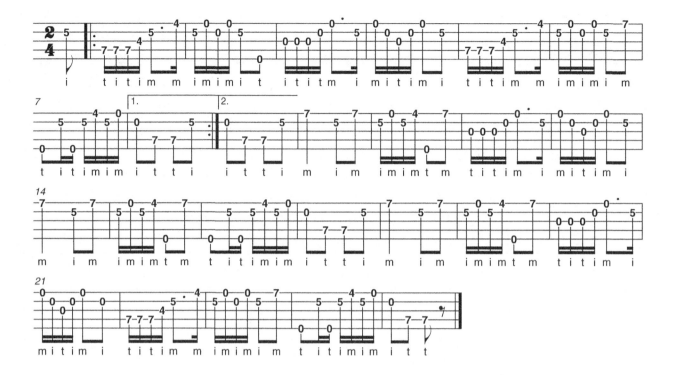

Johnny Cope

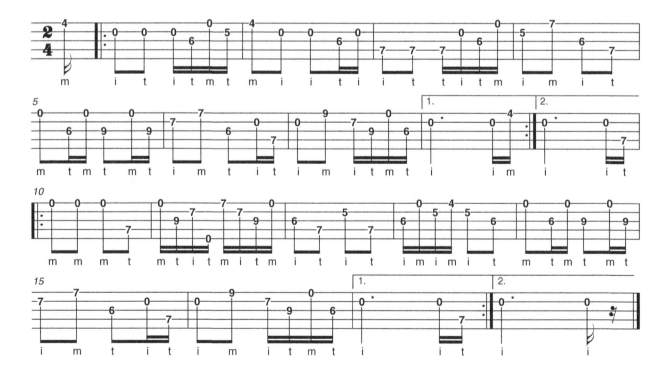

My Love She's but a Lassie Yet

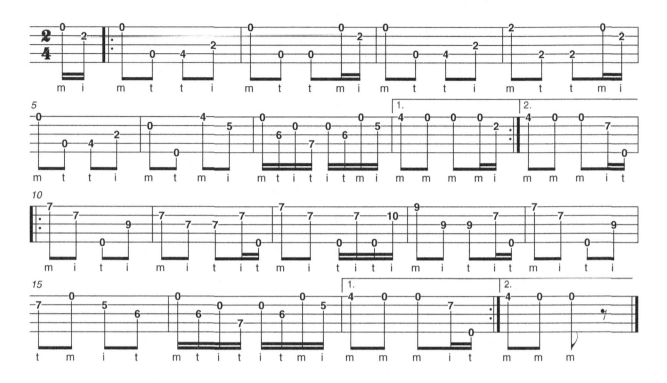

Lord Randolph's Bride

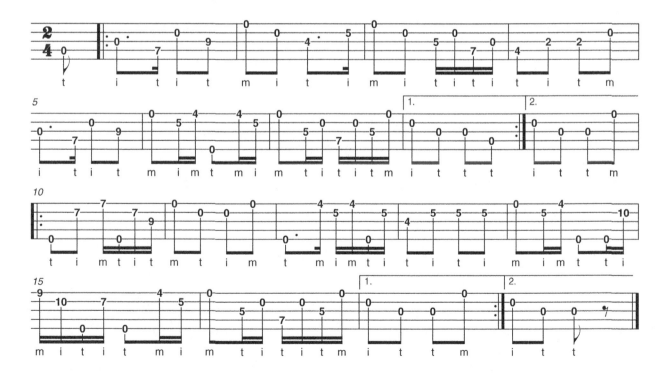

The Duke of Perth

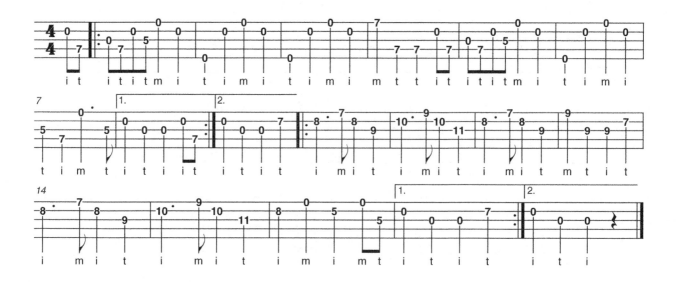

Lady MacKenzie of Coull

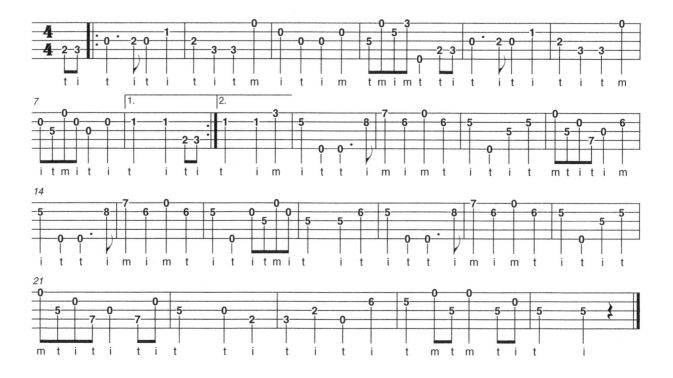

Glengarry's March

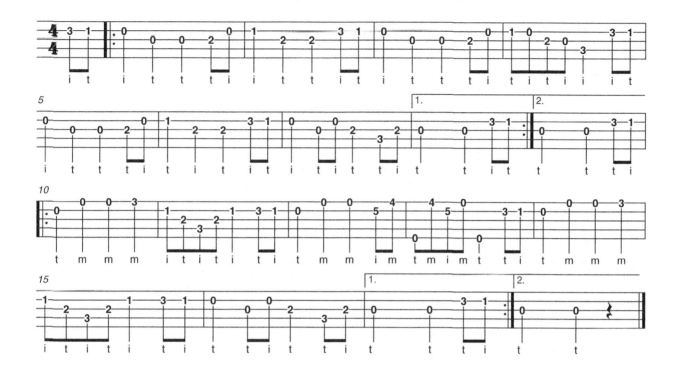

East Neuk of Fife

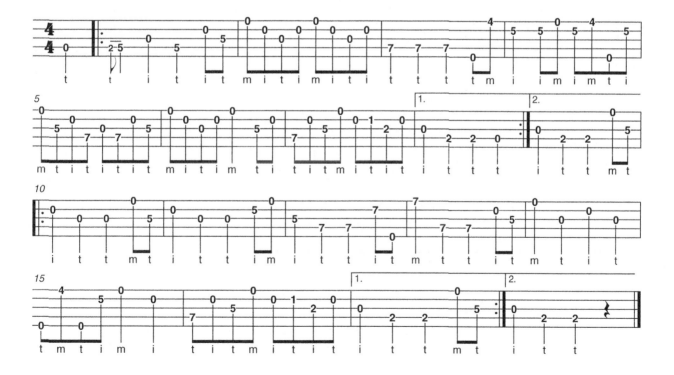

23

Jackie Coleman's Reel

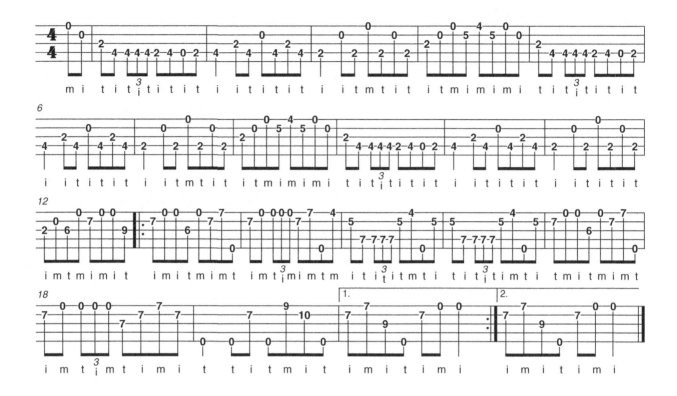

Drowsy Maggie

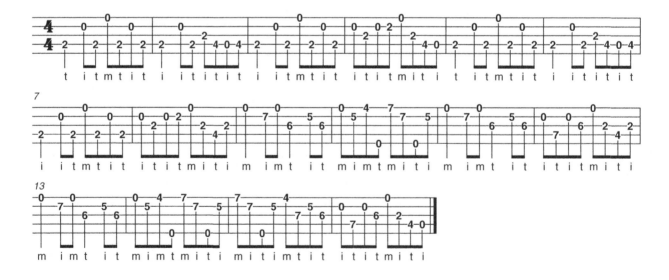

Willafjord

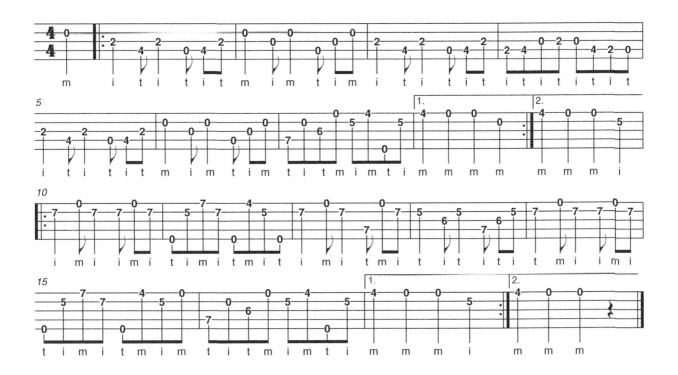

St. Anne's Reel

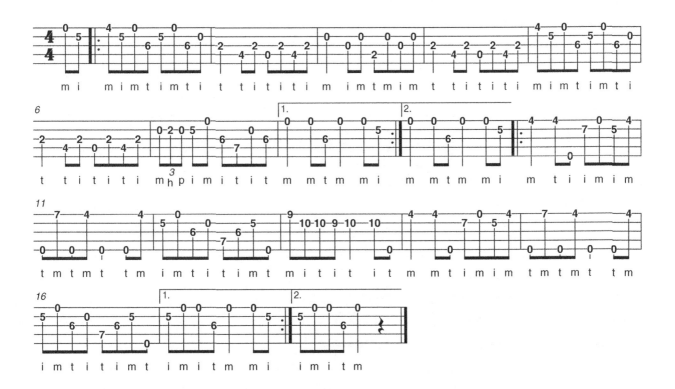

The Sally Gardens

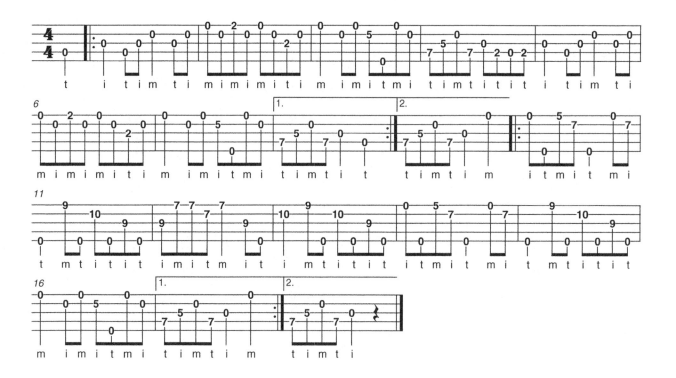

The Maid Behind the Door

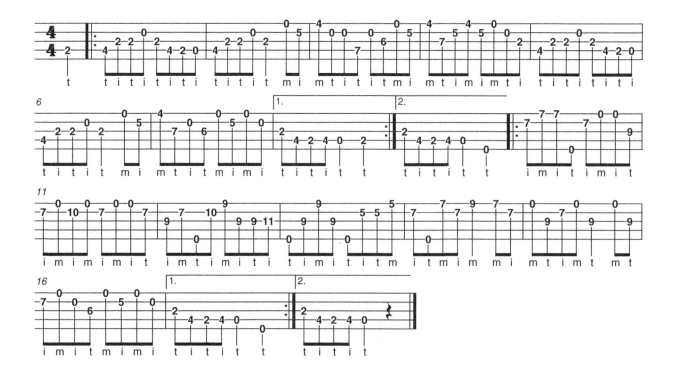

26

The New High Level

Composed by Andrew Rankine

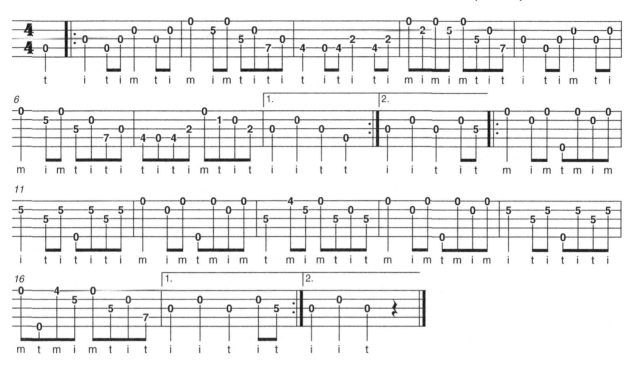

The Hamilton Rant or Dr. Bob Smith

Composed by J. Stanley Hamilton

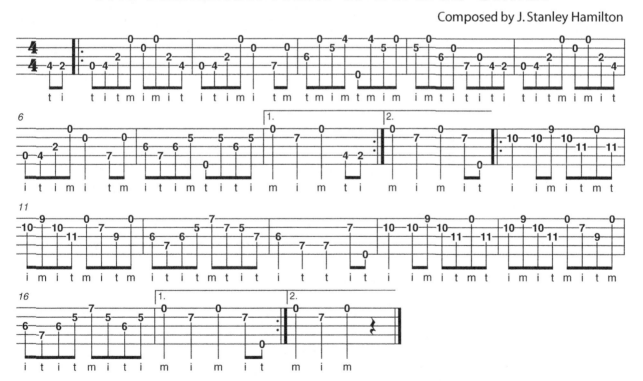

The Dashing White Sergeant

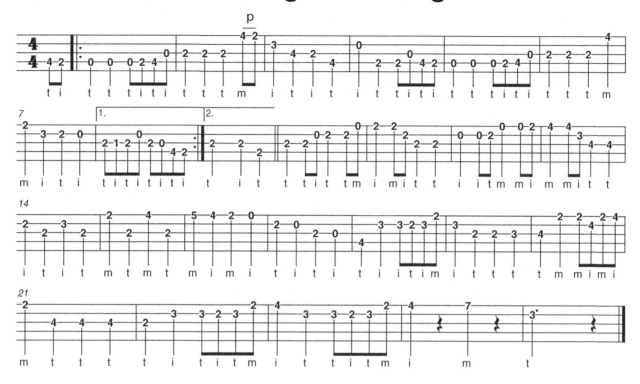

Niel Gow's Farewell to Whisky

Composed by Niel Gow

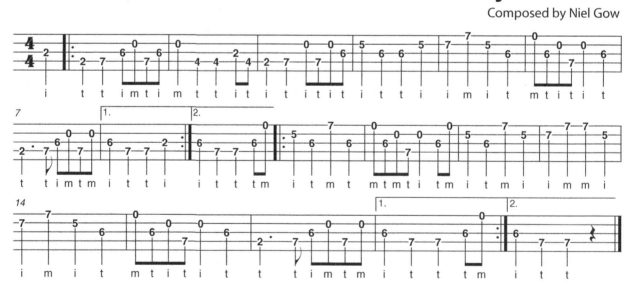

This Is No My Ain Lassie

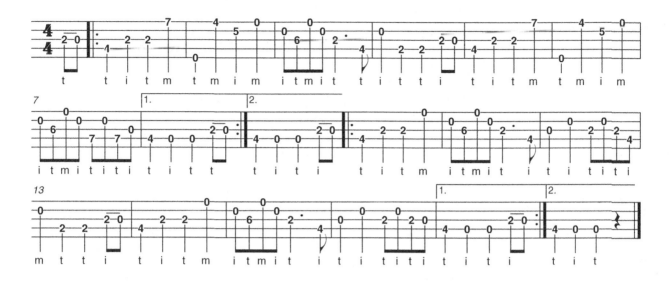

Bonnie Prince Charlie

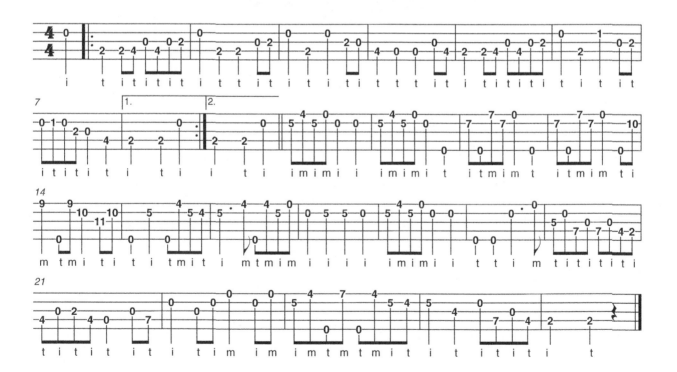

Jigs

Castle Lachlan in Strathlachlan.
The home of the MacLachlan Clan, which was destroyed in 1746 after
the defeat of Bonnie Prince Charlie

Shandon Bells

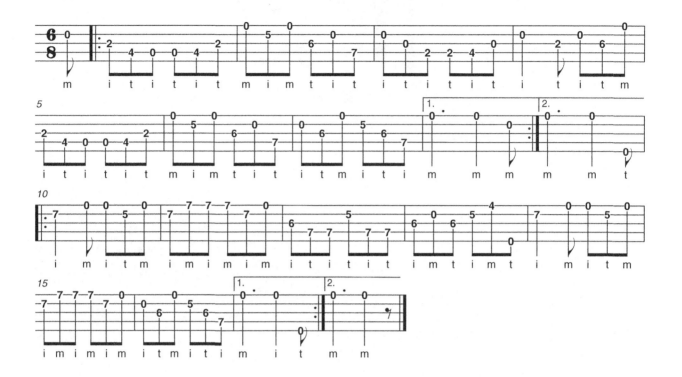

Sweet Biddy Daly

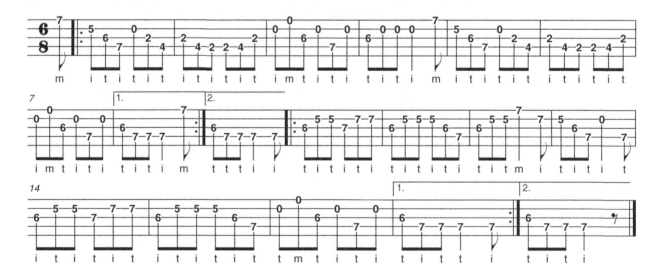

The Tenpenny Bit

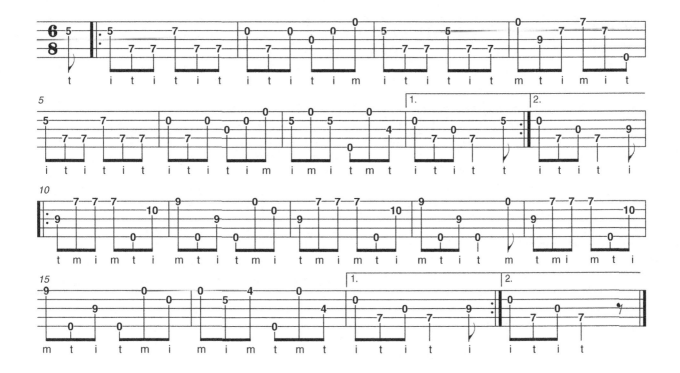

Humours of Glendart

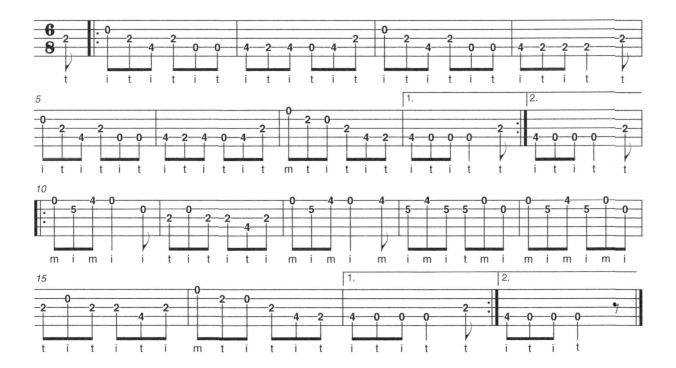

The Jig Run Rig

Composed by Fergie MacDonald

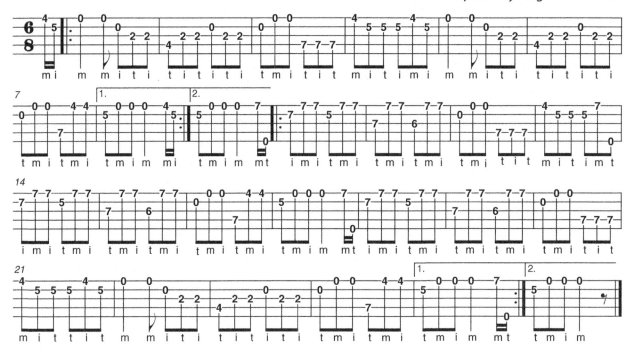

Scarce o' Tatties

Composed by Norman MacLean

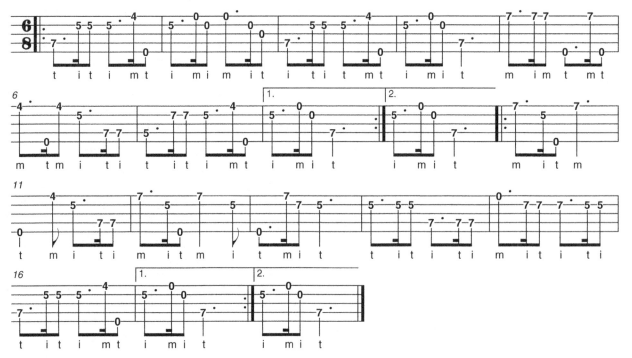

The Kesh Jig

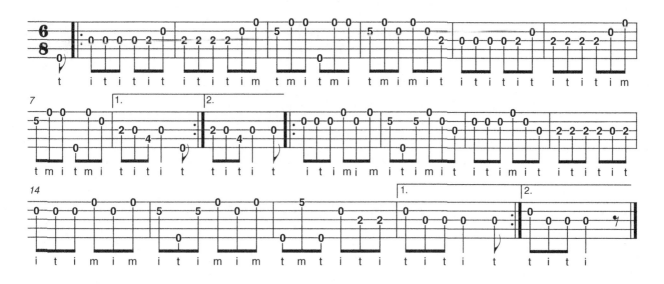

The Boys of Ballymote

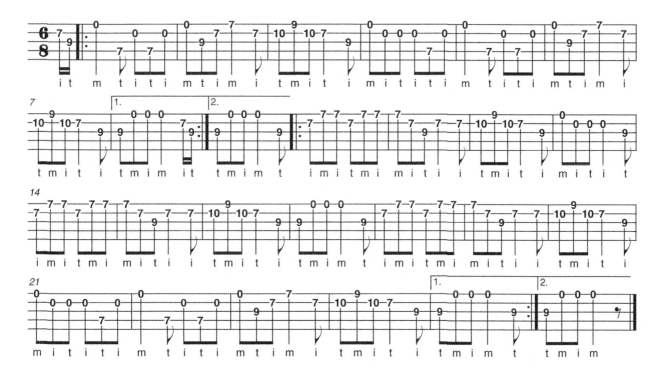

Swallowtail Jig

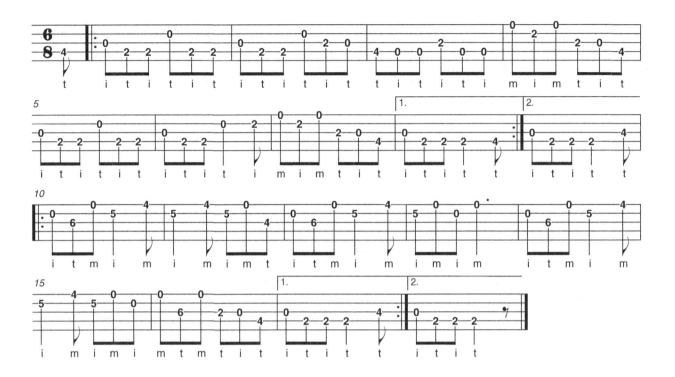

Corner House Jig

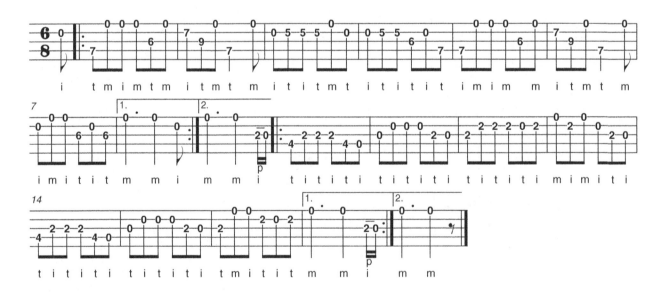

The Geese in the Bog

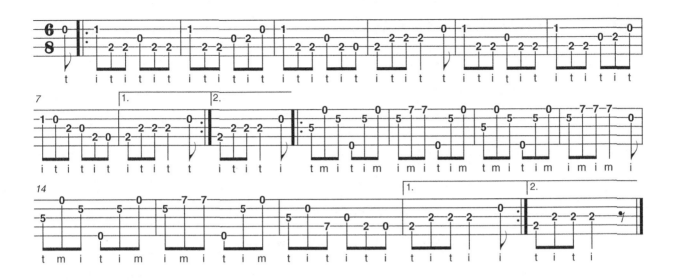

Morrison's Jig

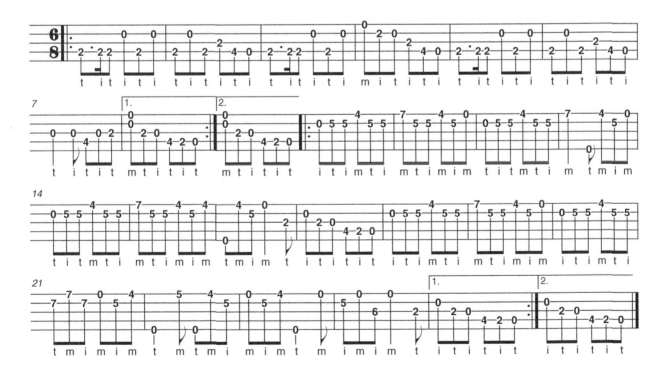

The Jig of Slurs

Composed by Pipe Major George S. McLennan

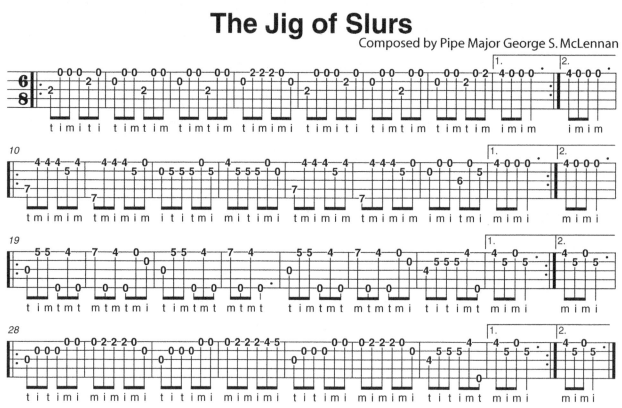

The Athole Highlanders

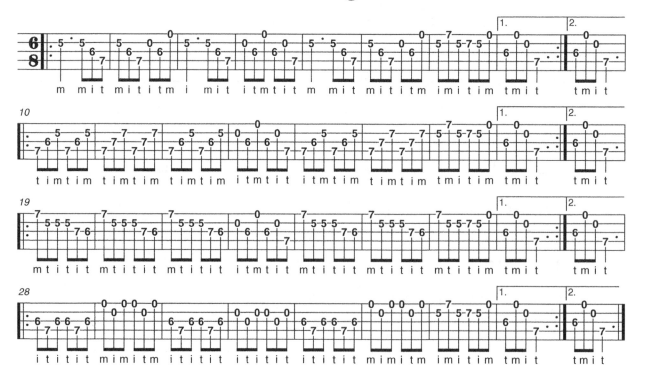

Paddy's Leather Breeches

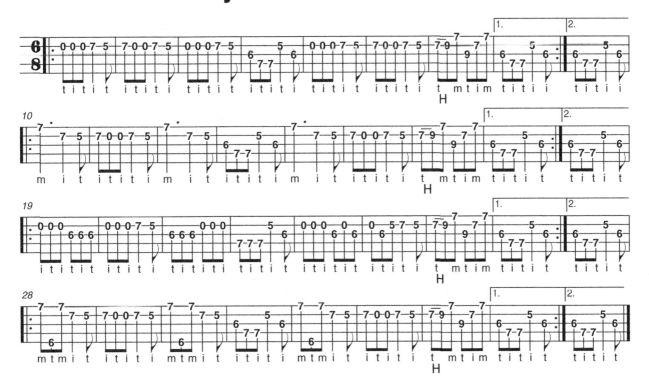

Lark in the Morning

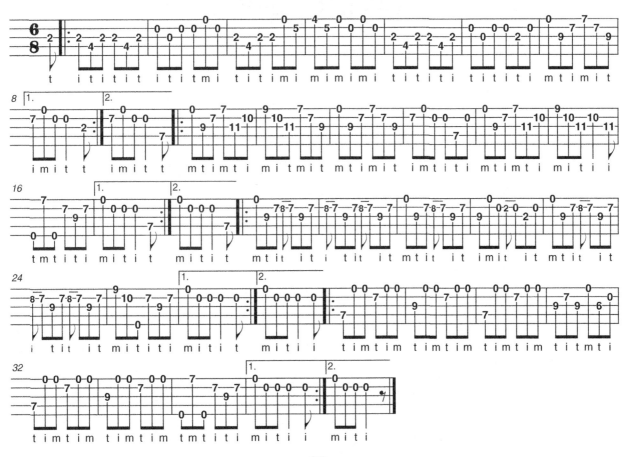

ꞏornpipes

The Cuillins on Skye

The Boys of Blue Hill

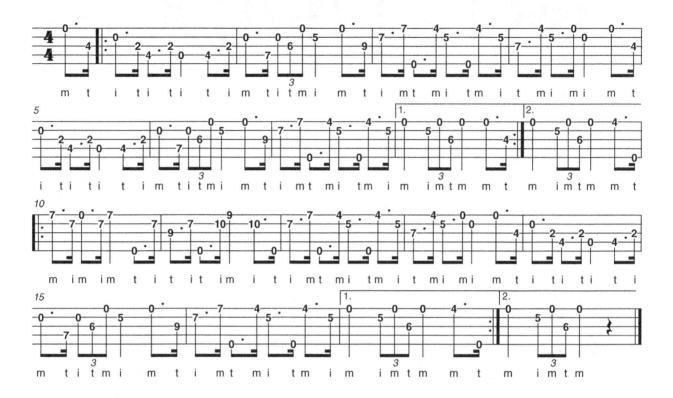

The Gypsies

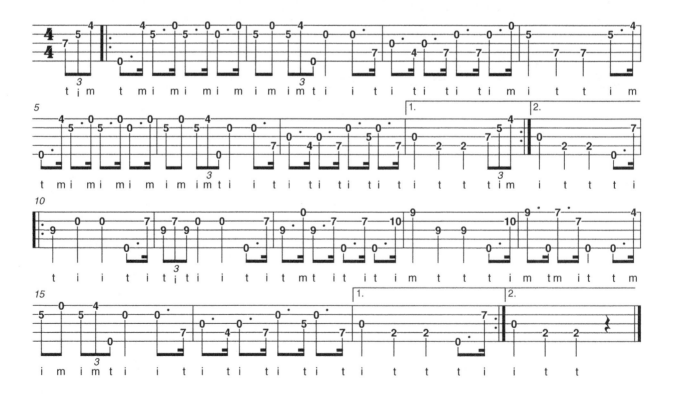

Chief O'Neill's Favourite

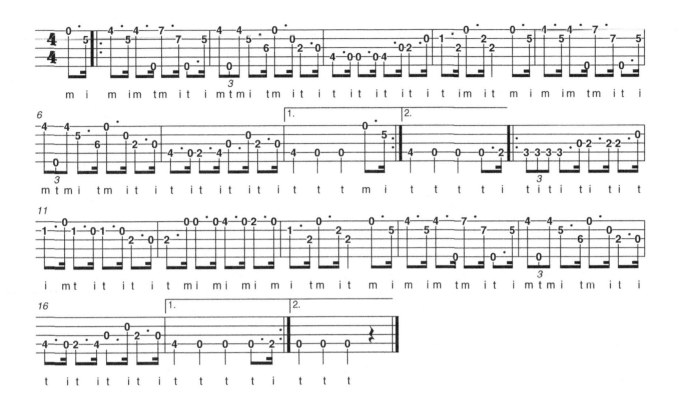

The Trumpet Hornpipe

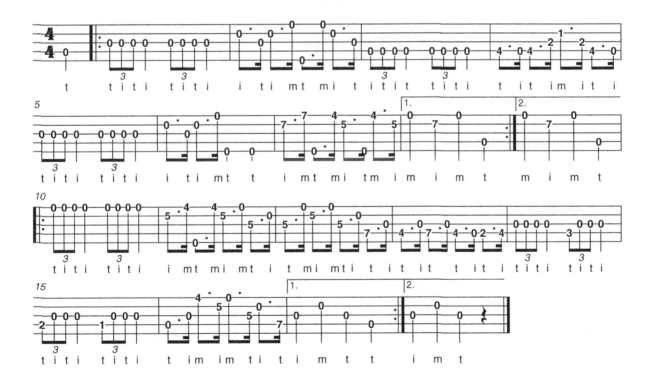

Marches

Urquhart Castle and Loch Ness

Scotland the Brave

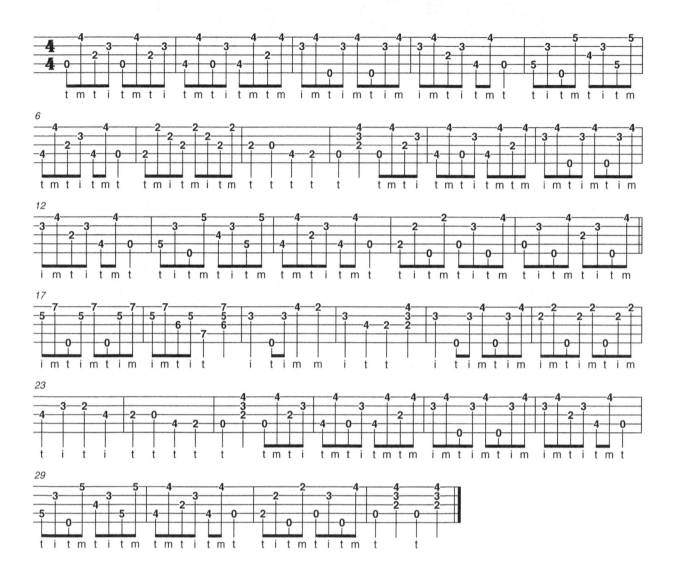

A Man's a Man for a' That

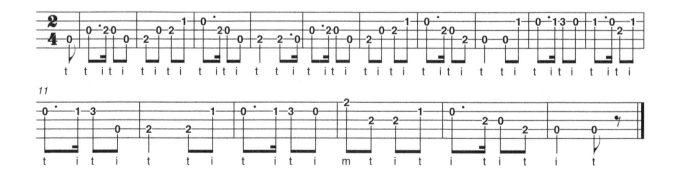

The Barren Rocks of Aden

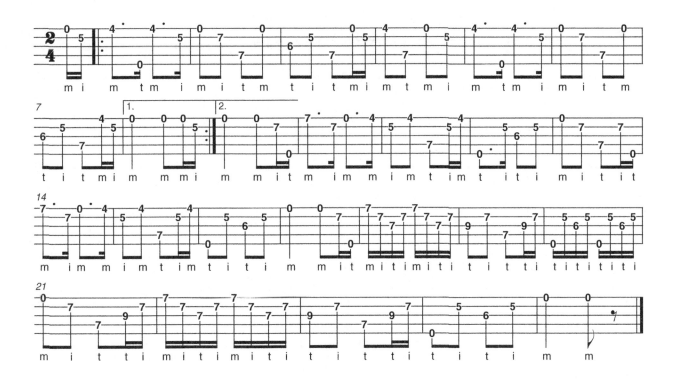

The High Road to Linton

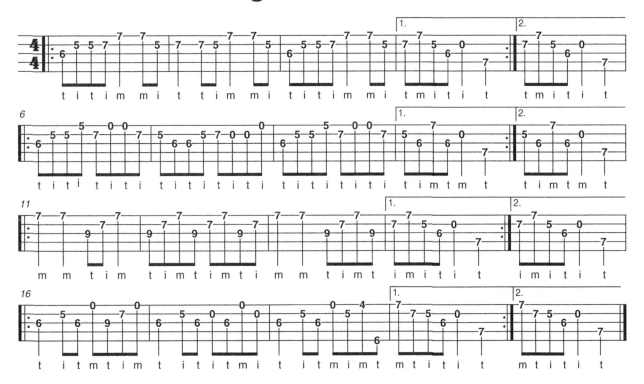

Captain Norman Orr-Ewing

Composed by Pipe Major W. Ross

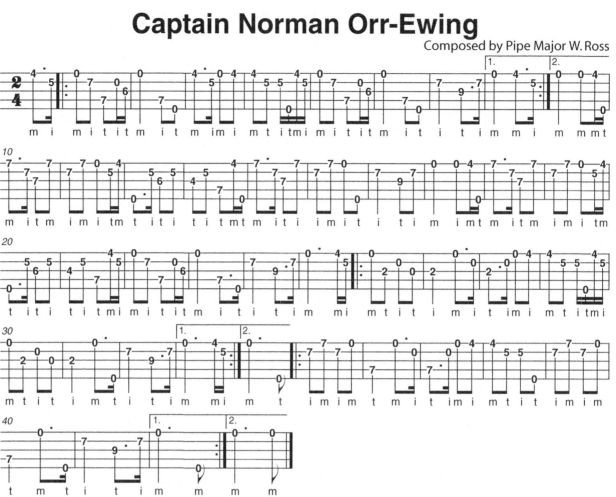

Flett from Flotta

Composed by Pipe Major Donald MacLeod

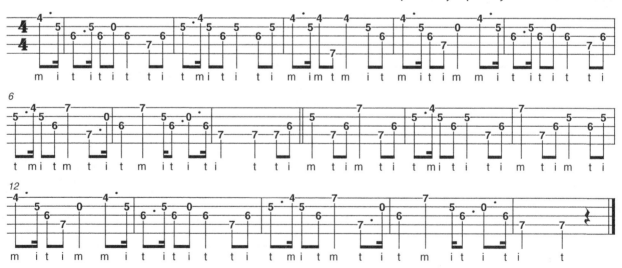

Pipe Major Donald MacLean of Lewis

Composed by Pipe Major Donald MacLeod

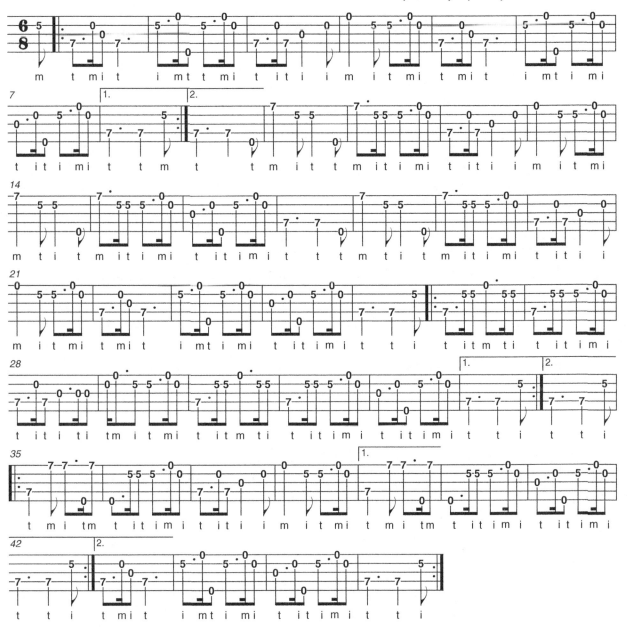

49

Pipe Major Jim Christie of Wick

Composed by Addie Harper

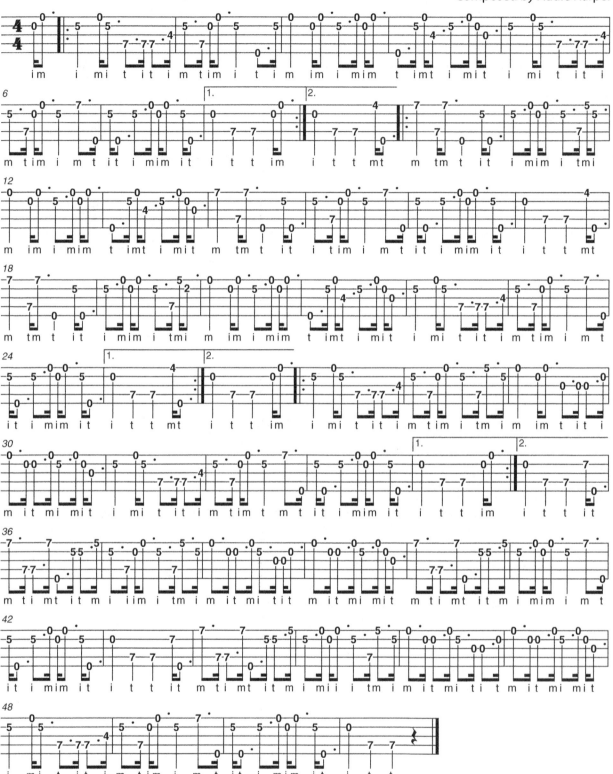

The Balkan Hills

51

Ballochgyle

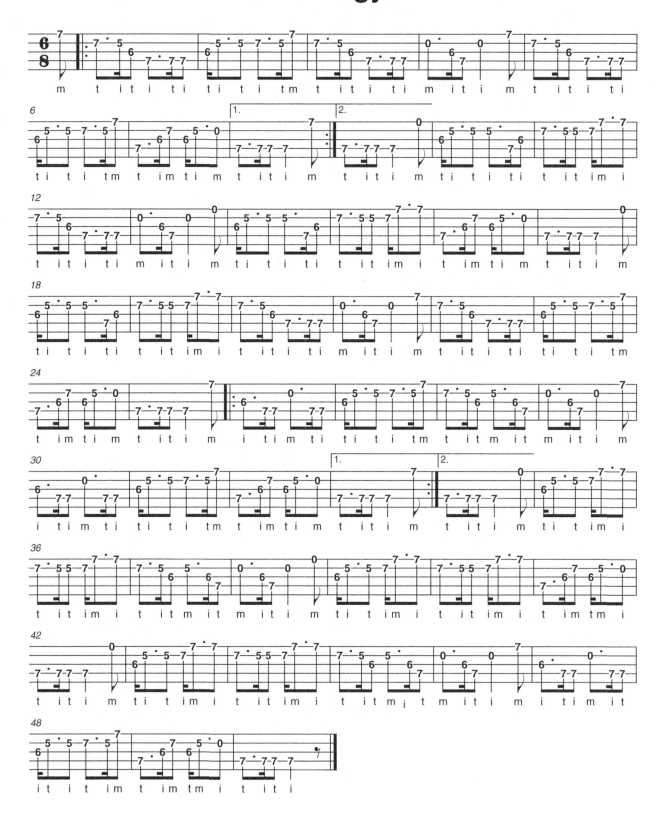

MacLeod of Mull

Composed by Pipe Major Donald MacLeod

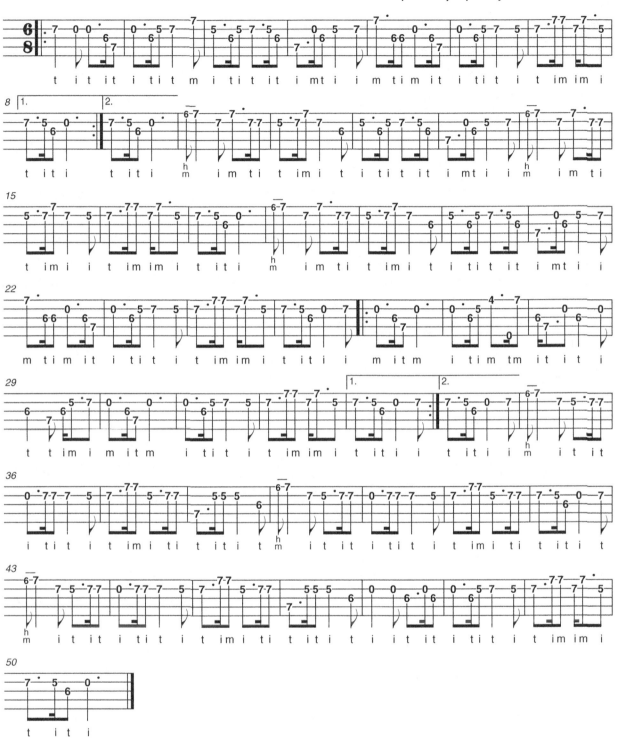

53

Glendaruel Highlanders

Composed by Pipe Major A. Fettes

Murdo MacKenzie of Torridon

Composed by Bobby MacLeod

The Man From Skye

Composed by Pipe Major D. MacLeod

Crossing the Minch

Composed by Pipe Major Donald Shaw Ramsay

Schottische

Fingal's Cave on Staffa

Loudon's Bonnie Woods

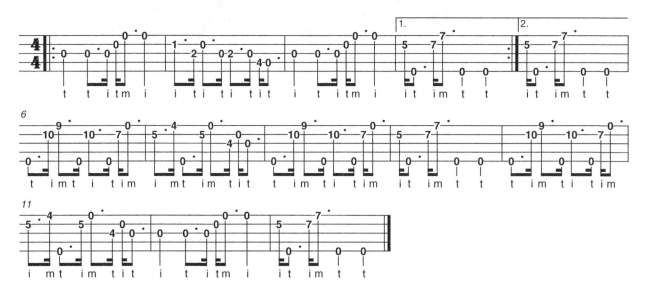

Kafoozalum

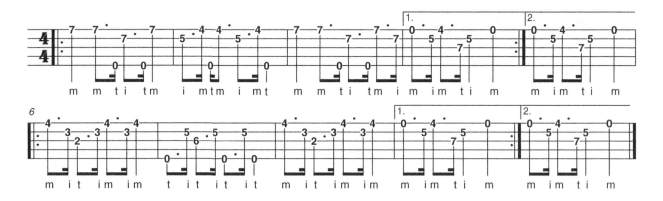

60

The Keel Row

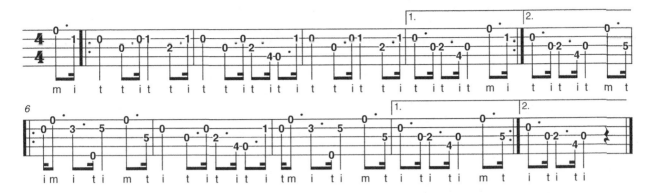

The Orange and the Blue

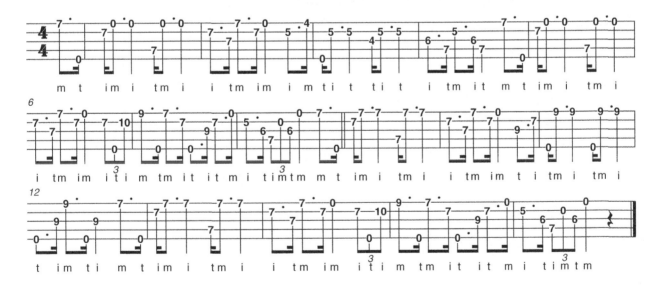

Two Steps

Blair Atholl

Shetland Two Step

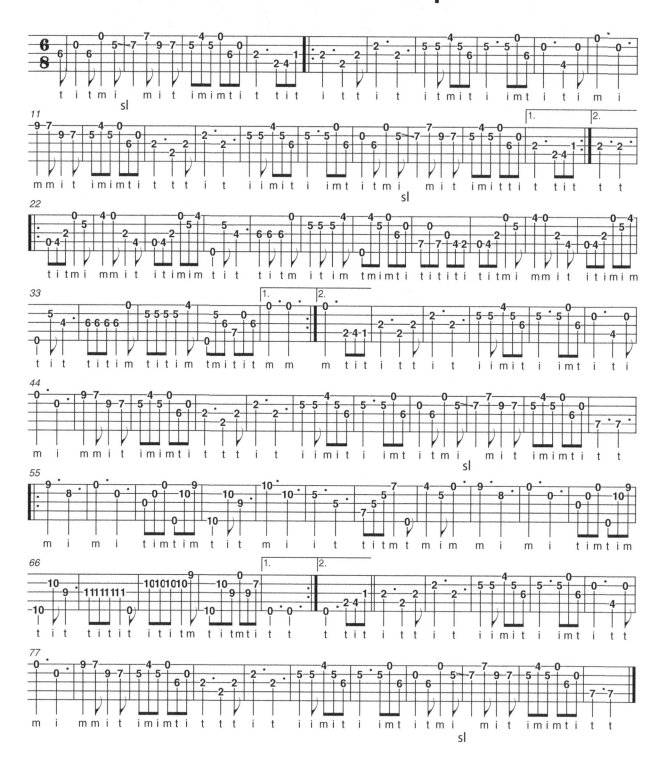

Looking for a Partner

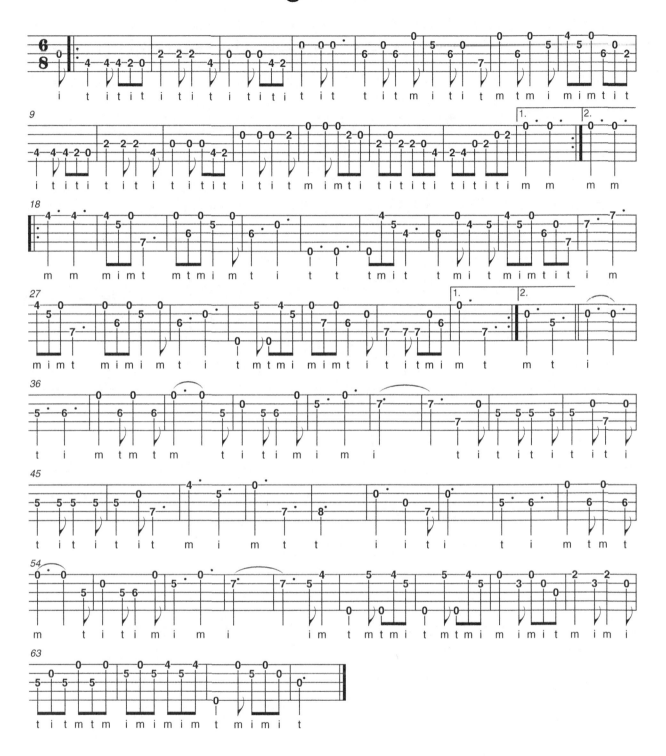

Frank Jamieson Two Step

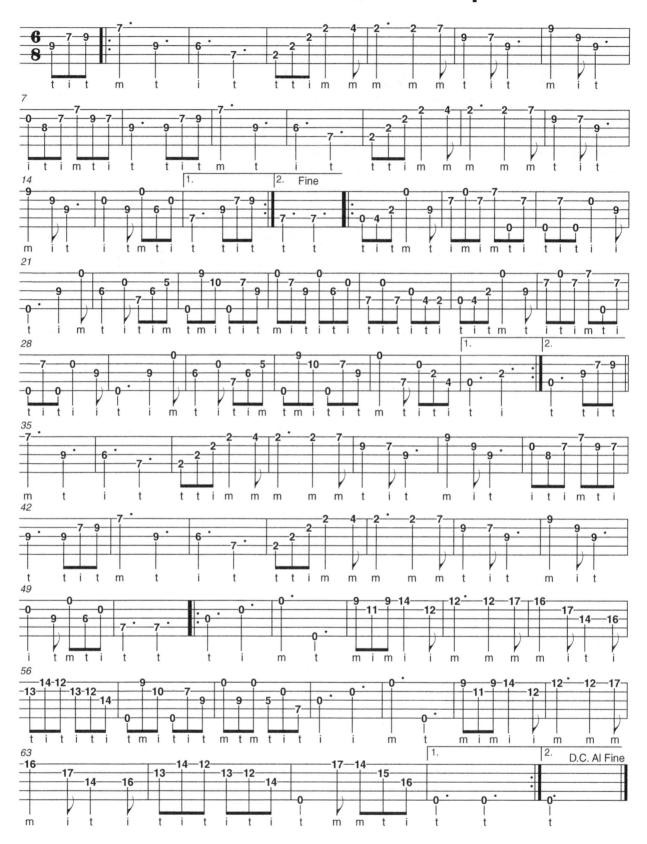

Polka

A typical scene in the Highlands of Scotland

The Patchwork Polka - Melody

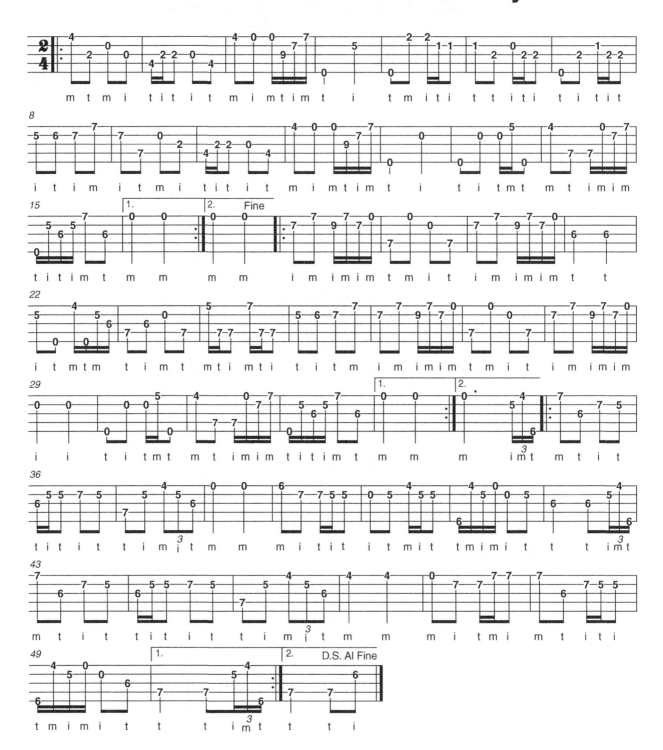

The Patchwork Polka - Harmony

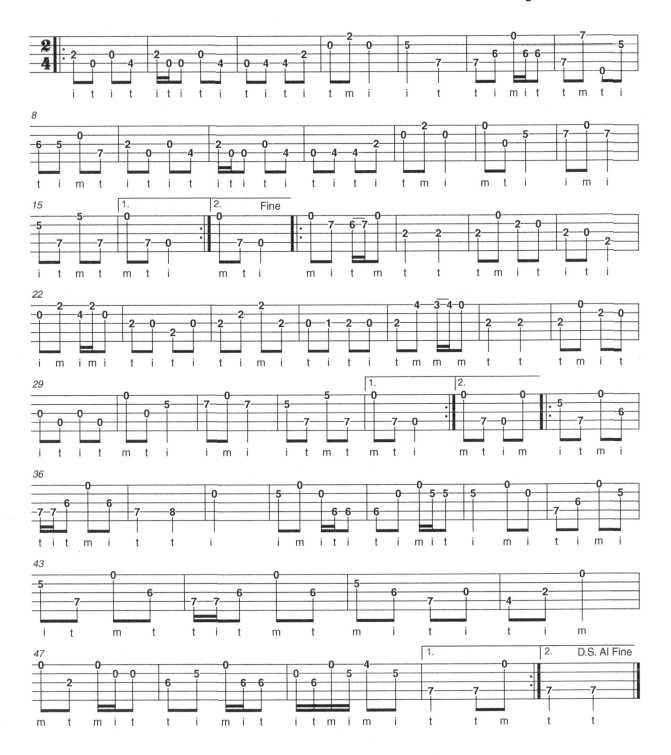

Waltzes

Standing stones at sunset

The Dark Island

Composed by Iain MacLachlan*

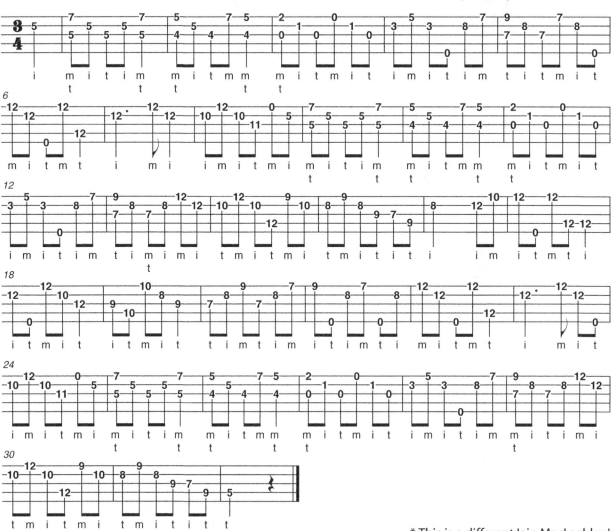

* This is a different Iain MacLachlan!
We share the same name.

The House of MacDonald

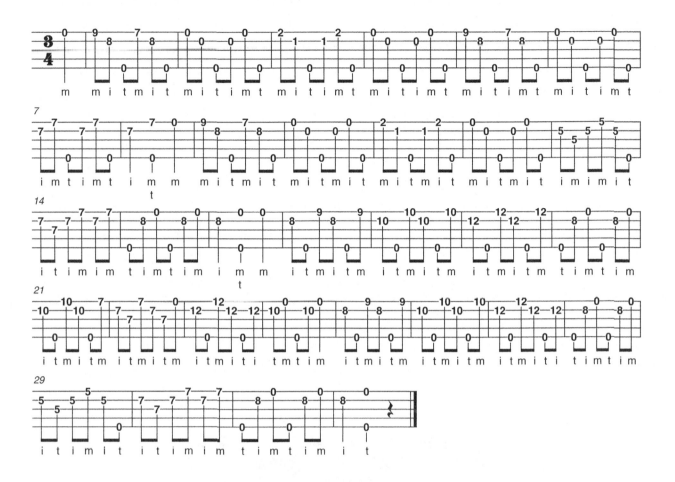

Strathspegs

Swans in winter in the Queen's Park, Edinburgh

Cameron's got his Wife Again

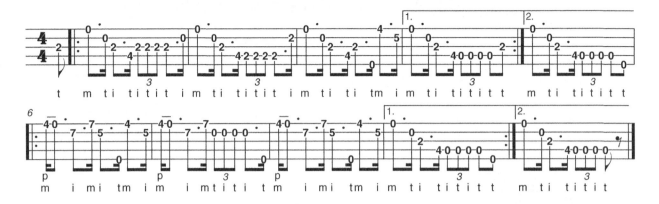

Highland Whisky

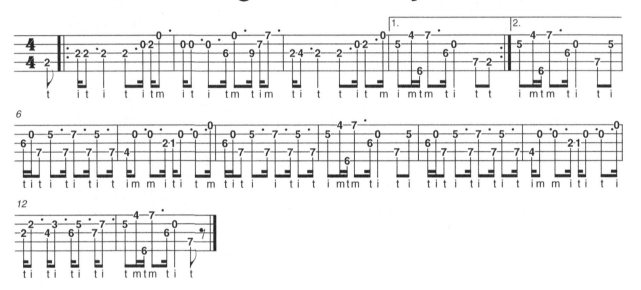

Jessie Smith

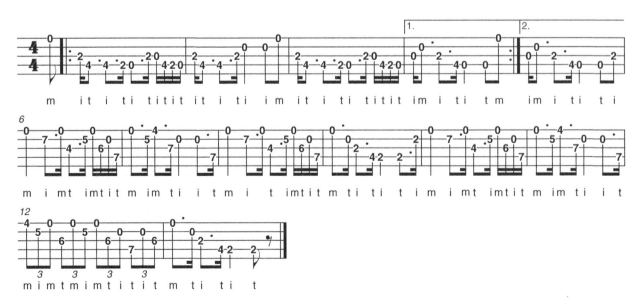

The Piper o' Dundee

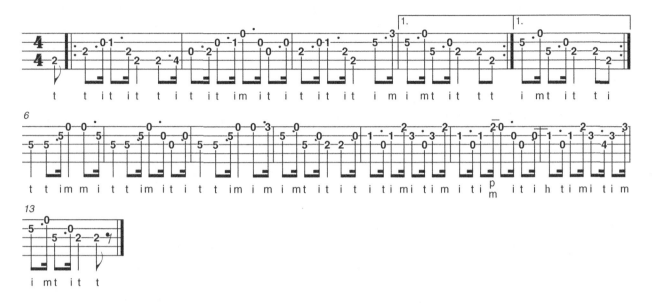

Iain and Tom Hanway comparing banjos in a pub in Longford, Ireland

March Strathspey and Reel

The Thunderdog Ceilidh Band
Iain MacLachlan, Paul Carline, Catriona Black, Phil Craig

The Sprig of Ivy

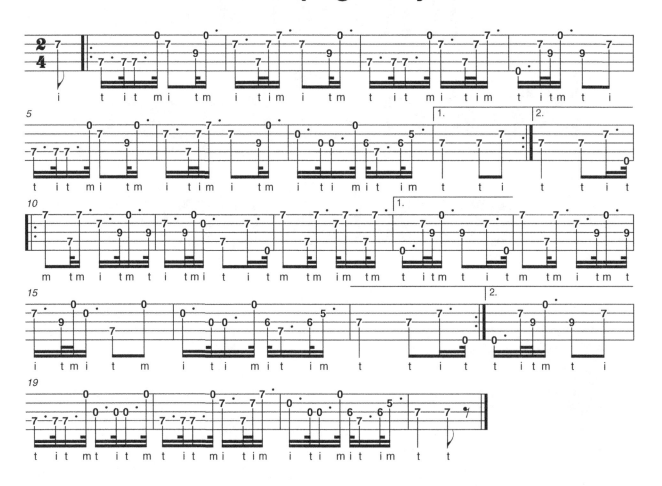

J F MacKenzie of Garrynahine

Composed by Pipe Master W. Ross

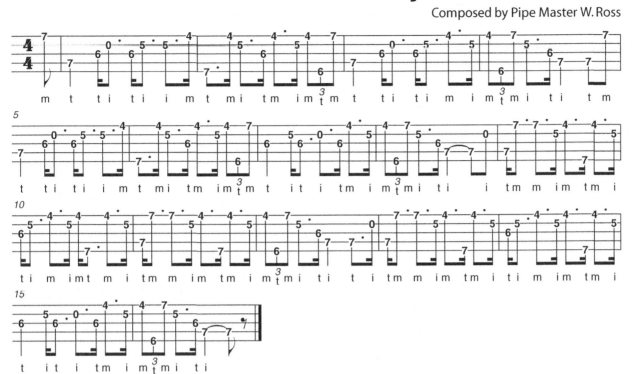

The Appletree

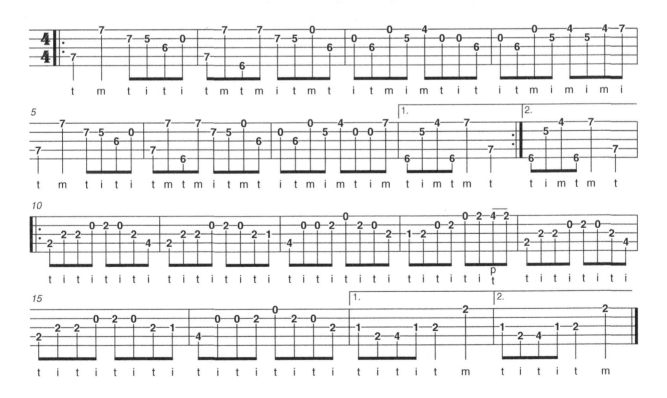

Extra Tunes

Dancing to the Thunderdog Ceilidh Band

Breakdown

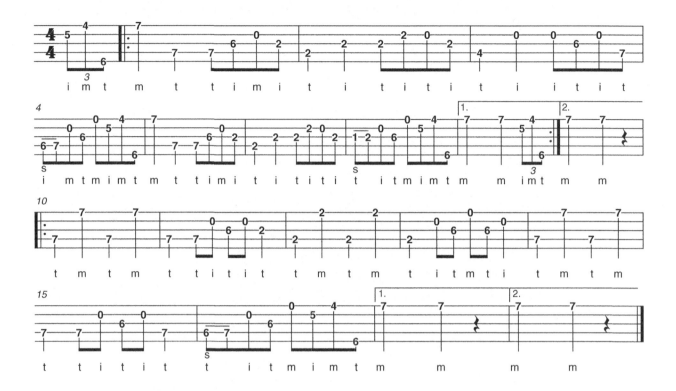

The Circassian Circle

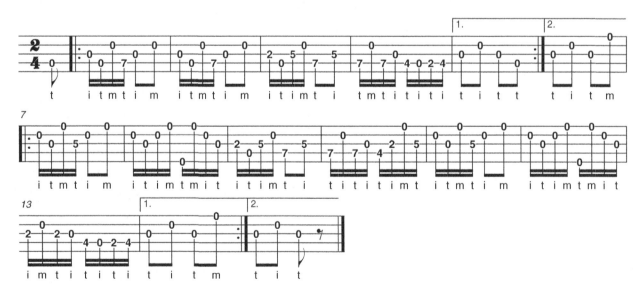

The Brolum

Composed by Dr. Charles Bannaty

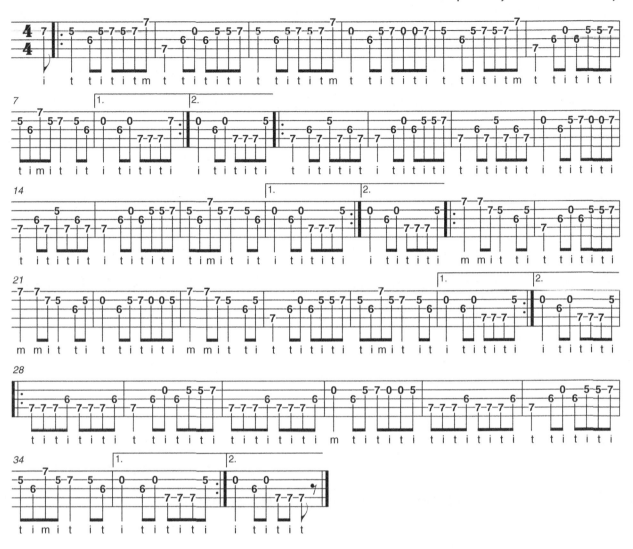

Jenny Dang the Weavers

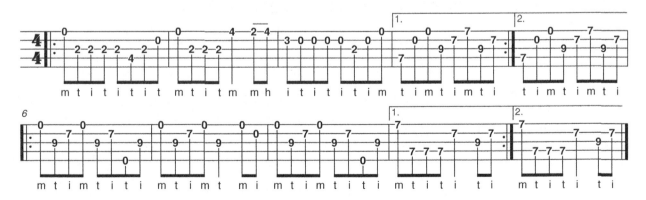

The Shetland Fiddler

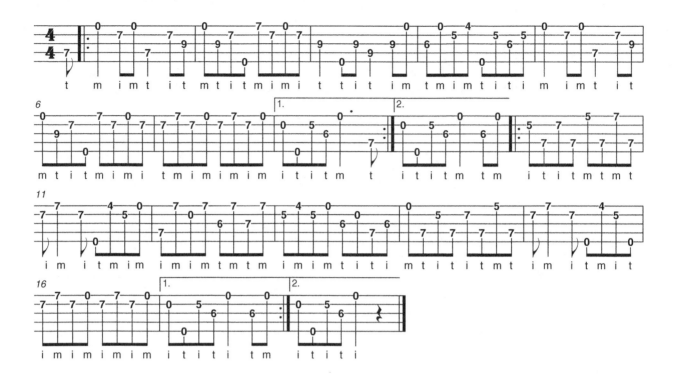

Lord MacDonald's Reel

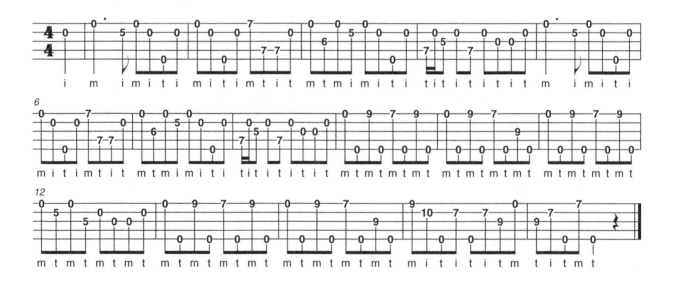

Sleep Soond Ida Morning

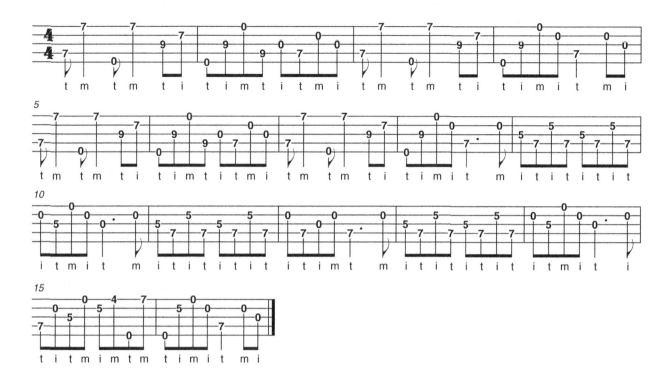

The Reconciliation

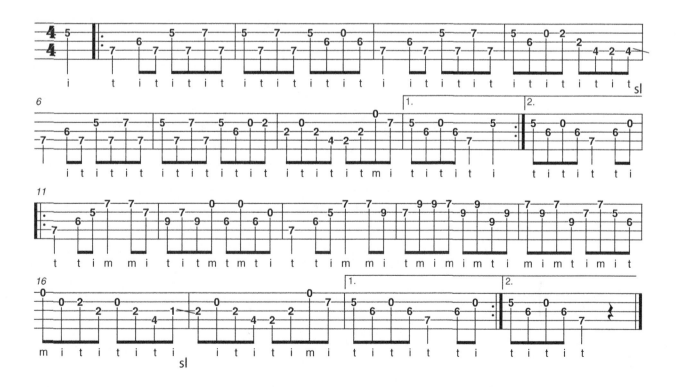

Tongadale Reel

Composed by Farquhar MacDonald

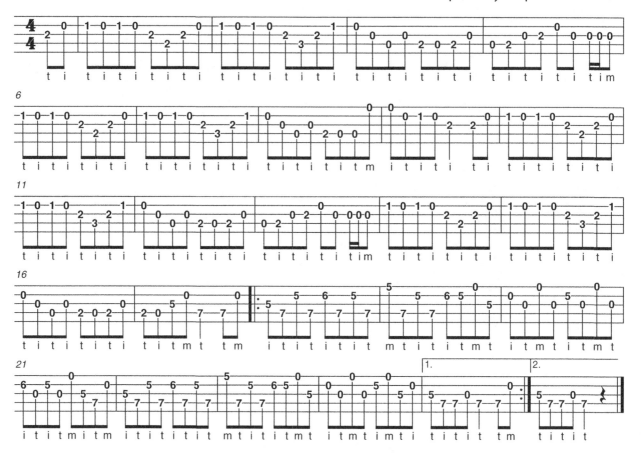

Rachel Rae

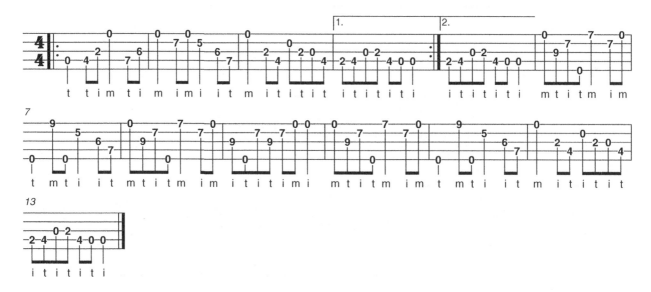

Goodnight and Joy be with You

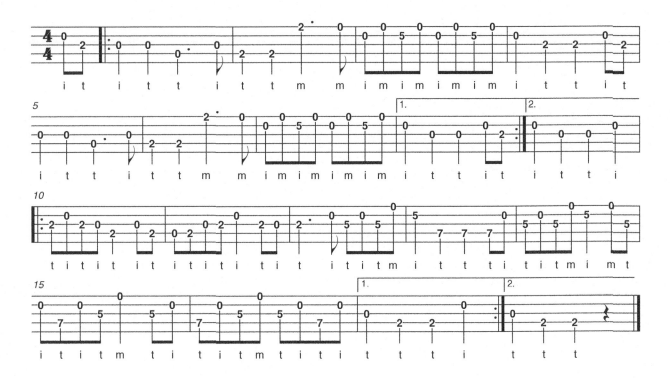

Tarbolton Lodge

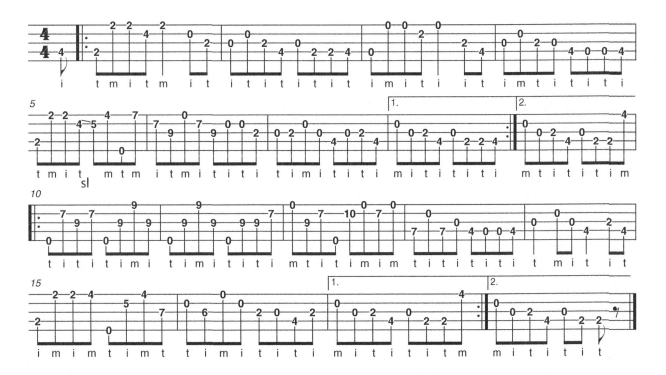

Haste to the Wedding

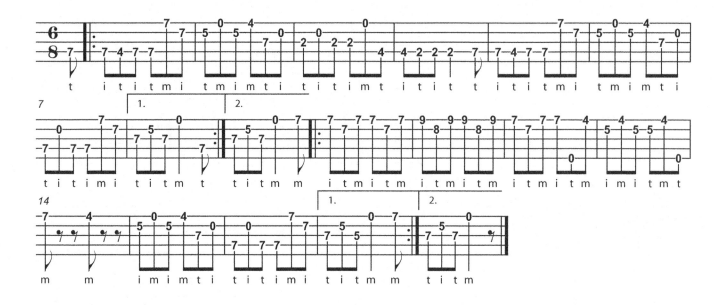

Skattery Island

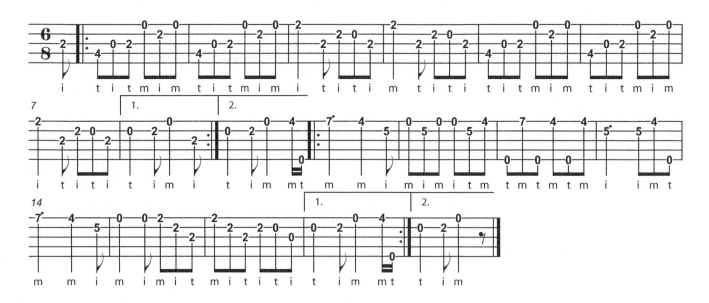

Bonnie Dundee

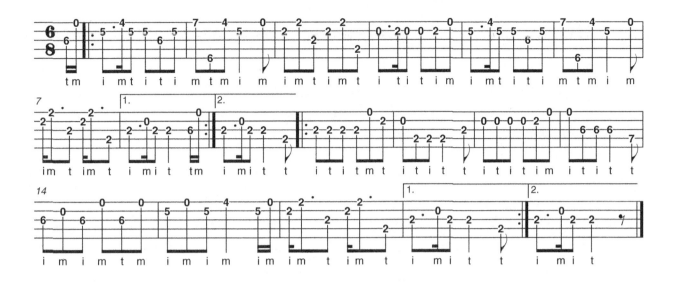

The Muckin o' Geordie's Byre

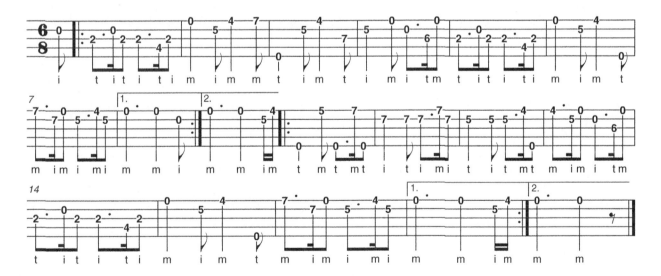

Aros Park

Composed by Alastair McKenzie

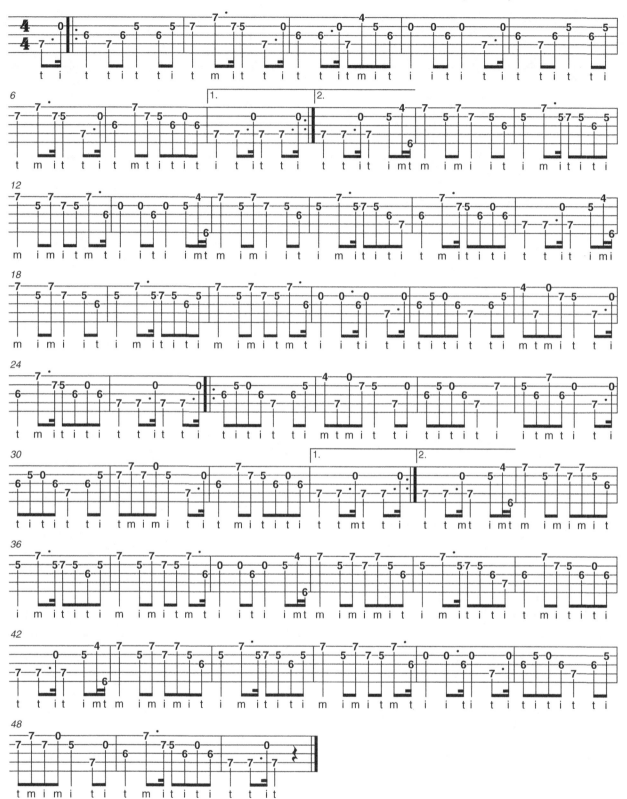

The Mathematician

Composed by J. Scott Skinner

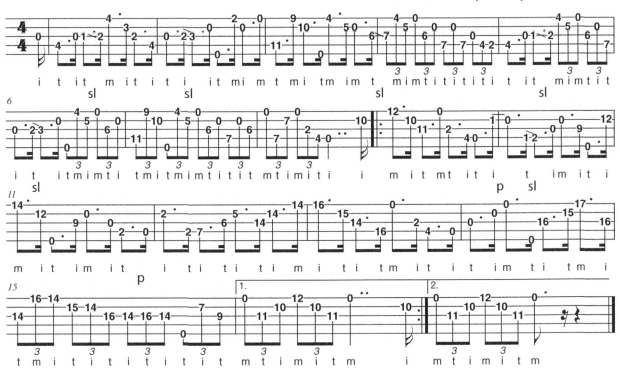

The Smith's a Gallant Fireman

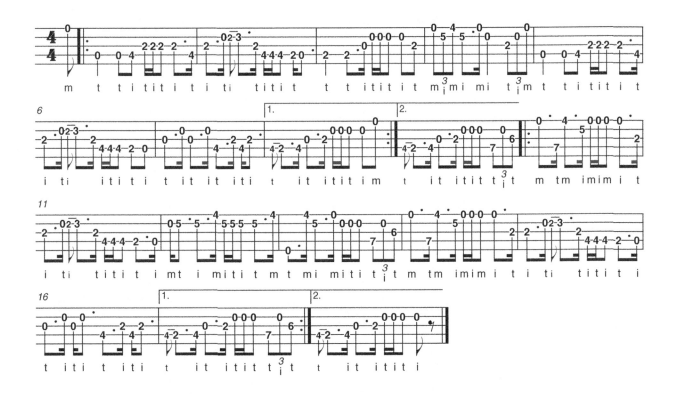

The Sweetness of Mary

Composed by Joan MacDonald Boes

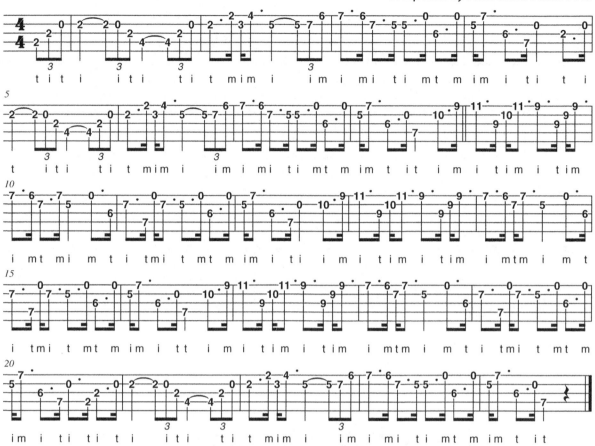

94

Loch Lomond

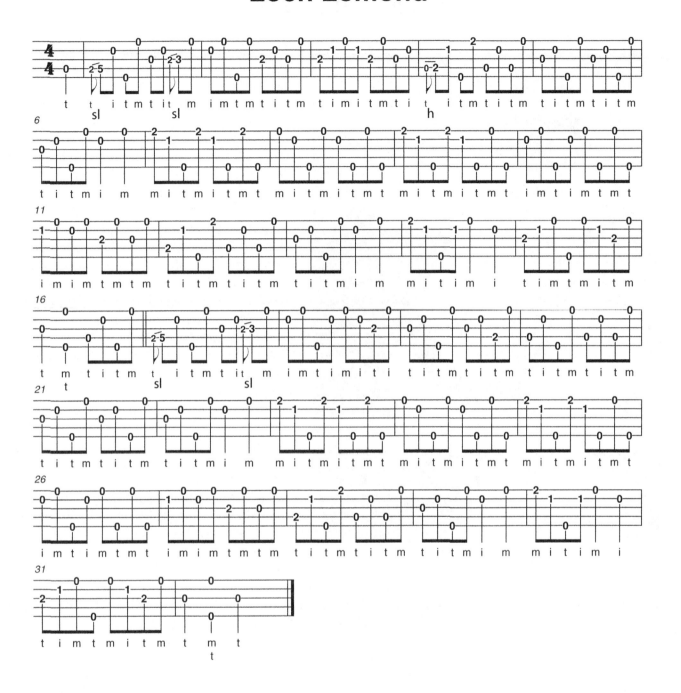

The Author

Photo by Marieke Smegen

I first started playing the banjo in 1968. I really came to it by accident rather than hearing it and thinking I want to do that. I had learned the cello while at school but did not keep it up after I left. I had taken up the guitar and was playing in a folk trio with my older brother and a friend from school. We all played guitar and sang Scottish and Irish folk songs. One day I decided that it was silly for us all to be playing guitar, as there was no variety in the sound we were producing. The next Saturday I bought a banjo. I knew nothing of banjos and couldn't even tune it. It was a long neck banjo but it did have 5 strings. I started off playing a 2 finger style. I played the tune with my thumb and my index finger playing the first string. It sounded a bit like banjo playing and I didn't really know any better.

The big change came one day when I was looking through the music in one of the local shops and came across the Earl Scruggs book. That event changed my life forever! It introduced me to a whole new world of banjo playing and has since taken me all over the country, to Poland, Germany and the USA. My two finger style was abandoned and the three finger Scruggs style became my Holy Grail. There have been many pitfalls on the way. Not the least of these was the fact that I had one of the early editions of the Scruggs book which had a number of errors. The most noticeable is that in the middle of "Shuckin' the Corn" the tune suddenly changes to "Farewell Blues". I still haven't mastered that!

In 1981 I formed a bluegrass band called Okefenokee after the swamp in Georgia. We got to be really good and made a couple of recordings, which we used to sell at gigs. We started playing for what we called Square Dances but what were really ceilidhs with an American flavor. This was where I met Colin MacLennan a very fine dance teacher who was calling the dances for us. In 1995 Colin was asked to teach a dance workshop for beginners ceilidh dancing. He wanted to use live music and asked if I would play for him. I pointed out that my knowledge of bluegrass banjo was pretty good but Scottish music for dancing to, was a different matter.

This didn't seem to be a problem to Colin so I got the job. Solo banjo for dance classes can't be very common but I turned up at the appointed hour. Things went well at first as I stood and played bluegrass. The dancers danced and Colin gave encouragement. However, we got to the point in the evening where the dance called for jigs. Who has ever heard of bluegrass jigs? Certainly there are none in the Scruggs book - not even hidden in "Shuckin' the Corn"! I had to learn fast. In this book you will find sets of jigs. They are fun to play and I think they work well on the 5 string. I have written a number of them for the band and hopefully you will add them to your repertoire.

Having played for classes for a year or so Colin suggested we get a band together. He was well known as a dance caller and lots of bands hired him for their gigs. He thought that it would be good to have his own band and be able to do the dances he wanted. As it happened in the class at that time was a friend of mine who is an excellent rock guitarist. In talking to Phil we found that he had just finished a spell as a bass player in a ceilidh band and was looking for a band to join. Paul joined on keyboards having never played ceilidh music before. Colin just seemed to have a knack of talking to the right people. Most Scottish dance bands include an accordion. We had already decided that we wanted to be different and not have an accordion so we were looking for a fiddle player. Once again Colin came up with a name of a fiddle player that he thought would be able to play with us. Joanne Slater is only half our ages but her fiddling is amazing. I have learned most of the tunes in this book from her and many of the sets were put together by her.

I had a lot to learn and so the tabs in this book were written. I take the tabs to gigs and read them as I play. Memorizing them is a slow process nowadays. Unfortunately my bluegrass band ceased to exist. The ceilidh band is so busy with work that I couldn't keep playing in both bands. I miss playing bluegrass but the challenges that I face nowadays on the banjo have been really exciting.

Made in the USA
Coppell, TX
11 April 2023

15481077R00057